STILL

A STORY OF SURVIVAL, LOVE, AND SECOND CHANCES

Charles Hamilton

Copyright © 2025 by Charles Hamilton

All rights reserved.

No portion of this book may be reproduced in any form without written permission from the publisher or author, except as permitted by U.S. copyright law.

"Some stories don't begin when you think they do."
-*Charles Hamilton*

Preface

This book is the culmination of years of surviving, questioning, and searching for meaning between silence and sound. I did not write to provide polished answers, nor to satisfy the shallow demands of history sanitized for comfort. I wrote to preserve the questions, the ones that linger, heavy and unresolved, in the places where memory collides with truth.

These pages are not only memoir, nor only reflection; they are fragments of pain and flashes of grace, scars and songs stitched together. They are proof that brokenness does not mean ending, and that to write is to bear witness, even when the world demands silence.

If you hold this book in your hands, you are already part of its story. Because none of us exists apart from our legacy, what I have lived through, you too may have glimpsed in shadows or storms. What you carry, I have felt in some other shape of grief or love. My story touches yours, because none of us survives alone.

And so, before you turn further, I want to open the door wide and tell you not just *why* I wrote, but *what* I hope you'll find in the pages ahead. Some call it spiritual peace; I always refer to it as *STILL*.

Introduction

This book is both a personal journey and a collective reflection. It is about survival, yes, but also about the questions that carve us long after the storms have passed.

Here, you will find my story, but I hope you will also find pieces of your own. You may recognize the fracture points, the unexpected silences, the fire that consumes, and the light that lingers. You may find echoes of your heartbreaks or your beginnings, woven between the lines.

My hope is not that you walk away with certainty but that you walk away awake, to your story, to your legacy, to the stillness that waits even in the fiercest storm.

I've put everything that I am into this story, and now I give it to you. I thank you for taking the time to read about my life. Welcome to Still.

-Charles Hamilton

Contents

Preface	3
Introduction	4
Becoming Still	6
Life before Us	11
Before We Knew What We Were	23
The Fracture	31
After the Fire, Before the Light	40
The Diagnosis	53
When the World Went Quiet	57
The Ring That Wasn't a Ring	62
The Ring that Changed Everything	69
Acknowledgements	74
A Letter to My Younger Self	76
Epilogue – Still	78
About the Author	81

CHAPTER 1

Becoming Still

This is a story I never thought I'd have the privilege of writing, and one I never imagined I'd have to live. In a world slowly unraveling at its stitched seams, I often find myself outside, working in our back yard, shaping my vision of a quiet, sacred paradise. My little heaven on Earth. But even in that space, peace is not always promised. Sometimes the challenge runs deeper than aching muscles or sore hands.

Sometimes the Louisiana heat bears down like a punishing spirit, rising past one hundred degrees, pressing against my skin until my thoughts begin to drift. I often pause, worn, disoriented, and in the haze, I see shadows move. I hear something unearthly whisper my name, as if crepitation itself had taken voice.

The heat settles over me like unwanted cancer, unrelenting, invasive, and somehow familiar. The kind of cancer that once lived inside my body, threatening to end me with a twist or a turn. But even on the worst of days, the Louisiana sun pales in comparison to what waits for me at home. I'm talking about my soulmate. When she walks into the room, I am never the same.

She moves like a promise fulfilled, carrying a love so full it spills past the flawless curve of her lips. And when she speaks... oh my God! When she speaks, I hear harmonies, soft and sacred, like a song only my soul can recognize. I still struggle to find the words to describe what it means to walk through life with your best friend and your soulmate at your side.

I don't know how to define our love, because it refuses the limits of clever words or polished romantic phrases. It reaches beyond sentiment. We are more than a memory meant to be cherished, more than pages waiting to be stirred by breath. Our love is the frame that holds our entanglement. It is not decoration; it is a foundation. It is the shape that the truth takes when two souls decide to hold on, even after time, pain, and distance try to tear them apart.

We did not take the path of least resistance. Long ago, we broke up, and for more than fifteen years, we lived in the shadows of that separation. We both tried to redefine love in the arms of others, but nothing ever felt whole. Nothing ever spoke the language of our souls. But look at us now. She is my sunrise, and every evening, she curls beside me like the warmth of dusk folding into my bones.

These days, I wake each morning with her scent stitched into my skin. She smells like morning roses. And together, we carry the fragrance of a rose by another name, familiar, eternal, and reborn. I love telling this story because she is every beautiful part of me made visible.

When our friends see us together, they often smile and say they can see our love, and that we're beautiful, magnetic, and made whole in the space of each other. And maybe we are. Perhaps we are everything that they see. But what they don't see is what it took to stand here, hand in hand. If you saw us now, you'd never guess that not long ago, the stench of death lingered just outside our door, waiting, watching, and whispering that our story was over before it had the chance to begin again.

* * *

Not long ago, I had cancer, and my spirit was caught in this bottomless chasm of hopelessness. I remember falling, deeper and deeper, into a darkness so thick it felt endless. Somewhere in that silence, I heard my father's voice calling me home from the grave, a voice both familiar and terrifying. In my confusion, I couldn't hear God. I strained to listen to his whisper, but all I could make out was the endless ringing of death's phone call, echoing louder each day.

I had become so tired, tired of the pain, tired of not knowing. Tired of feeling like I'd been left behind by everyone, especially the ones who promised they'd stay.

The thought of death became almost comforting. It offered something that life no longer could: absolution, peace, and a reunion with my mother and father in a place where pain couldn't follow. I wore a ring, but I was abandoned by the very ones entrusted to care for me. The person closest to me, the one I thought would stand beside me, told me she was tired of hearing about my cancer. She needed a break. And just like that, I was alone.

My life had collapsed into a cold circle of concern, a hollow echo of what care once meant. So, I moved forward, not because I was well, but because I still had the strength to walk with integrity. I moved on, sick, destitute, but not defeated. Looking back now, I realize I was broken then. I was left to rot in the silence of that betrayal. In my heart, I had made peace with death. I was ready to face God's judgment. But He... God would not open the courtroom doors.

As fate would have it, one day I was talking with my cousin Brandon when he asked a question that froze me in my tracks. "Have you told her?" He was referring to her, my estranged soulmate. I shook my head. I told him we hadn't spoken in years, and I didn't want to burden her with my problems. I was dying, and I didn't want to place that weight on the one person I had once loved more than life itself. But Brandon didn't hesitate. He took it upon himself to leave a note on her door, telling her the truth. At the bottom, he wrote: "He could use a friend."

A few days later, the phone rang, and my heart nearly stopped. Her voice spilled through the line, trembling and cracked, like it had been broken by time but still knew how to find me.

"I heard you're in trouble," she said.

"I am," I answered softly.

"I want to see you," she whispered, and I said yes.

But truthfully, I was terrified. Terrified, she'd see how much the disease had taken from me. Afraid she'd see death clinging to my skin like a second shadow.

Despite everything, we met. When I saw her again, all the years disappeared. And the first words that left my mouth, fragile and trembling, were: I love you.

My lips were weakened by illness, my body barely holding itself together, but the words came from the strongest part of me. They came from my heart. I cried as I spoke, the weight of fifteen years crashing down inside those three syllables. I felt the crash because I was still in love with this woman. Even now, as I write these words, just the thought of her makes my heart scream and my hands shake. That's how deep she lives in me.

When we met again, she didn't see the cancer. She didn't flinch at the sight of my pain or the shadow of death trailing behind me. She reached for my hand and never let it go. After fifteen years apart, she looked at me like no time had passed. Like love had been waiting patiently for us to return.

In time, I beat the cancer. And I got back the love I had never stopped praying for. But our story didn't begin with survival or reunion. It began more than eighteen years ago, when two souls first recognized each other across the distance of a lifetime.

This is our story. And this... is Still.

CHAPTER 2

Life before Us

This is not a love story in the traditional sense. It's a story of survival, forgiveness, rediscovery, and the kind of love that doesn't die even when everything else seems to. My name is Charles Hamilton. I wrote this not only to honor her but also to understand the man I had become before she returned.

Before we met, I was a former writer who had laid down his pen and pad in pursuit of a normal life. I still remember why I chose writing over relationships. In the beginning, I believed God was shaping my voice for a greater purpose.

But somewhere along the way, my writing became so consuming that it placed me in a kind of emotional vacuum, a space where I lost sight of who I was and how I saw myself. It was a chamber of isolation. And yet, that solitude became sacred.

It eventually taught me how to empathize. It deepened my spirit and forged a quiet bond between me and the stories I researched. In that silence, I became a better listener.

But as the years passed, something inside me began to shift. I started to crave a deeper connection with the people closest to me. Not because I was lonely, at least, not in the traditional sense. It was more like... a hunger to evolve—a yearning to explore what came *after* purpose.

I hoped to find someone like me, a kindred spirit. Someone who shared my values, my desires. Someone who wanted more than what the world could see.

I had spent what felt like a lifetime in public life. So, I was never truly alone. Yet, at the same time, I always was. That's the paradox. Surrounded by people. Adored, yet somehow... unseen.

Still, I held on to hope. A quiet, stubborn hope that someone, somewhere, would see past the image. Past the applause. Past the title. I longed for someone who would want the man behind the name, the version of me that the world didn't see.

Because those two selves, though forged in the same fire, were not the same. One was built for admiration. The other was built for love, and if I'm honest, I've had my chances to love, and I failed.

※ ※ ※

I married my childhood sweetheart at the age of nineteen. We were young, wide-eyed, and filled with the belief that love alone could carry us through. But childhood love is fragile; it relies on dreams and fades when tested by reality. I wasn't a good husband. I was proud, distracted, and arrogant. In the end, I hurt someone who didn't deserve my carelessness. We had a daughter, and the marriage unraveled within three years.

At first, I hardly saw my child. I had become something else entirely, a personality, a brand, a man who lived for lights, sound, and recognition. Somewhere in all that performance, I stopped being a father. That descent will always live inside me, and that's something I acknowledge. I'm not proud of it. But strangely, I've come to be grateful for the failure because it taught me that love ends when purpose is misplaced.

On one side of my life were people, relationships, intimacy, and connection. On the other side was the work. And I was married to the work.

I've always wanted my writing to shift the world's axis. I wanted to change how people saw themselves. But I knew I couldn't do that by staying on the surface. I had to become the words embedded in the hearts and minds of people. I had to live between the blank lines and empty spaces. I had to disappear into my purpose.

To achieve this, I sacrificed, again and again, until my life became the work. Until birthdays were forgotten. Until dinners grew cold. Until the quiet moments, the ones meant to be shared, echoed in a home built by solitude.

Eventually, I sacrificed the career itself. Not because I was finished, but because I was tired. Tired of giving the world everything and returning home to nothing. Tired of being loved for what I created, but not for who I was when the pages stopped turning.

So, I walked away. I traded those blank lines and empty spaces for the so-called American Dream. I gave up the fire in search of a quieter belonging. I wanted something that couldn't be bought or published. I wanted a place to rest. To be held. To feel what it meant to be loved for simply being me.

But transformation isn't gentle. Reinventing yourself can be painful, and ironically, success can make you less hirable. I was forced to become someone smaller than the version of me I once celebrated, and even worse, I had to pretend that I was okay with that. I had to lie to my reflection.

I used to take my thoughts and breathe them into form. I used to speak and watch entire ideas take flight. But now... I was just a man looking for a job.

Still, I made that choice because I was starving to be loved for who I was in silence, not for what I could do in public. That decision led me down a difficult, unfamiliar path. When the music faded and the lights went dark, a different kind of light appeared, and my path became clear.

The hardest part was adjusting to a world of limitations. I'd never believed in ceilings, but now I was surrounded by people who did. And slowly, their limitations became mine. I began to shrink. I started to question the very essence of who I was. I felt like a fish out of water, drowning in clean air.

For years, my writing called to me. It whispered like a former lover, begging me to come home. And to me, it was a lover, one that raised me, shaped me, whispered truth in the quiet moments. But the whispers faded. And I let go.

The transition was brutal. When I walked away from that life, I lost everything that had once defined me. The bells. The whistles. The applause. I became ordinary. And even when I found myself in relationships, I felt empty. Because I was still unseen, and then... I saw the boat.

It was drifting down the Mississippi, quiet, steady, gliding like it belonged to another world. And something in me stirred. I looked at it and knew: That's what I want to do.

I wanted to become a boat captain. The idea sounded wild. The odds were laughable. But I've never been one to let the size of a dream scare me. I got a job on the docks as a barge washer, six dollars a barge. On a good day, I made twenty dollars. The days were long. The labor was hard. But for the first time in years, I felt alive again.

Eventually, I worked my way into the office. When I told my boss I wanted to become a captain, he laughed in my face. But I didn't laugh back. I simply moved on.

I found another company, and there, I did it all. I worked on the boats during the day and in the office at night. Most times, I stayed awake for 60 hours straight, working, and then crashed for twelve hours, and started it all again the next day. I did this for three years. Not for glory. Not for status. But because I was chasing a life that felt true.

I wish I could say I rose entirely on my own, that I built this life with nothing but grit and resolve. But the truth is, I wasn't alone.

Somewhere in the middle of my becoming, a family took me in. Not out of obligation. Not as a cause. But because they saw me, before I fully saw myself. They loved me quietly, without fanfare, and with a steadiness that still humbles me to this day. Their presence offered me something I didn't know I was searching for: a place to belong. And through them, I learned that sometimes, the softest hands shape us the most.

In time, I earned the title I had long pursued. Captain. The stripes, the wheelhouse, the weight of responsibility, it was mine. After years of breaking my body against the edge of ambition, of pushing past exhaustion, past sleep, past anything resembling balance, I had finally arrived. But when I stood there, at the helm of that vessel, I felt a strange and sobering truth: I didn't know how to drive the boat.

In all my focus, all my sacrifice, I had forgotten to prepare for what came after the goal. My hard work had opened the door, but my inexperience stood waiting at the threshold, asking if I truly belonged there. It didn't feel like failure. It felt like an invitation to start again.

The training didn't come from manuals or schools. It came from long-forgotten friendships, men I'd shared pool tables and quiet wisdom with, who now offered guidance from afar. One encouraged me to apply to a marine placement company. I still remember that interview. I was sitting across the table, saying with complete honesty: "If you send me out now, I'll probably lose the job in a month. But give me one more chance, and I'll last twice as long."

And that's how it happened. With every river, every harbor, every whispered instruction from voices I trusted, I began to find my way. I had reached the helm, but I was still learning how to hold it.

I thought peace would come with the title. I thought I had finally made it to the stillness I'd been chasing. But something unexpected followed.

Women began approaching me, not for the man I was, but for the idea of me. I was pursued not with intimacy, but with projection. And though I tried to stay guarded, eventually, I gave in. I married a woman who was still tethered to a man who no longer lived in her home but still occupied her heart.

The sun didn't rise on that union for long. We smiled for photos. We told the world we were fine. But behind closed doors, silence settled in like dust. You can't help who you fall in love with. But you can feel when love does not fall back.

I remember the day I came home after working away for over fifty days. I was exhausted, the kind of tired that lives in your bones. It was just after six in the evening. The neighbor across the street was outside cutting her grass. The air was thick, the sky dimming. I walked through the door expecting warmth. The smell of dinner. A kiss. Something soft. Something safe.

But the house was cold. I remember saying, "I don't feel loved by you." And I remember her response. Nothing. In response, I had made an offhand comment, "I bet that woman across the street would appreciate a man like me." She didn't flinch. Didn't argue. "Then go get her," she said. And in that moment, something shifted. Quietly. Permanently.

When the marriage ended, I didn't shout. I didn't beg. I wrote my number on a piece of paper, folded it carefully, and slipped it into the neighbor's mailbox. I had no idea what would come next. But I knew I was ready for something real.

※ ※ ※

I didn't expect a response. Honestly, I wasn't sure what I was hoping for. Maybe closure. Maybe curiosity. Maybe… grace. But a few months later, the phone rang.

It was evening again. I was in one of my quiet moods, the kind of quiet that comes just before the sky gives up its last light. The house was still. The TV was off. And I was sitting alone, lost in thought, when her voice reached through the silence and found me. There was a pause. Then—

> *"Hello. You left your number in my mailbox."*

She said, her tone laced with something fragile. Something unsure.

> *"Are you divorced?"*

"Yes," I replied, steadying my breath as best I could. Another pause. But this time, it wasn't hesitation; it was *weight*. The kind of silence that holds meaning. The kind that feels like an unopened gift between two people. "Would you like to go to dinner?" I asked, barely above a whisper. And just like that, the air shifted. Time softened. My pulse slowed.

I didn't know what this would become. I didn't know if it would be a conversation, a coffee, or the first spark of something I had almost stopped believing in. But I knew one thing. For the first time in a very long time…I felt seen.

Two days later, I woke up feeling unburdened by simple truths. My mind was clear. For the first time in a long while, I knew what I wanted. Or at least, I knew what I didn't want; I wasn't looking for a fleeting moment or just a date to pass the time. I didn't have a map for what came next, but I knew I wanted more than a few pleasantries and polite smiles. I wanted something that felt alive.

※ ※ ※

We agreed to meet at six. It was ten in the morning when we set the time, which meant I had exactly 480 minutes to unravel in quiet panic.

I tried everything I could think of to stay busy. Cleaned. Paced. Showered. Changed clothes. Then changed again. But nothing could distract me. My nerves were on fire. My palms were sweaty, my skin clammy, and my heartbeat echoed like a drumline in my chest. I felt like a sixteen-year-old boy on his first real date, somewhere between thrilled and terrified.

The clock ticked on, each second louder than the one before. Time slowed and sped up all at once, like it knew something I didn't. Still, I got into my car and drove the grand distance of 200 feet.

Yes, she lived just across the street. I told myself I must be crazy to date someone who lives in my neighborhood. I mean, what happens if this goes wrong? What if she sees me taking out the trash after heartbreak? And then... the door opened.

She stepped outside like the dusk had saved its light just for her. Glowing. Effortless. There was something sacred in the way she moved, as if even time held its breath to watch her walk. Her beauty wasn't loud or showy. It was still. It didn't demand attention; it invited surrender.

When she opened the car door and slipped inside, I braced myself for what she might say.

Her first word? "Hello." Just that. And I... forgot how to speak. My lips went dry. My hands clenched the steering wheel like it might fly away. I felt my bones tremble. This was going to be one of *those* nights.

A short while later, we arrived at her favorite restaurant. The atmosphere was warm, dim, almost dreamlike. Fish tanks lined the walls, glowing with soft blue light. The water shimmered like it was breathing. The kind of place where the world slows down just enough for truth to show up.

I walked behind her like a bodyguard, pretending to be calm. I tried not to stare, but it was impossible. She was the kind of beautiful you couldn't ignore, elegant, confident, every movement deliberate yet soft. The kind of woman who didn't try to steal attention but had already taken it before she spoke.

We sat down, and before the water glasses even hit the table, she leaned in. "What do you want from me?" she asked. I blinked. "Do you just need someone to talk to?" I started to answer, but she wasn't finished. "Are you looking for a friend? Because I already have friends."

She stared straight through me, like she could see the space where my intentions lived. She wasn't playing games. She was opening the door to something real and daring me to walk through. I don't remember exactly what I said in response. Maybe I didn't say much at all. Maybe she didn't need an answer just yet...

After dinner, I didn't try to kiss her. I didn't need to. That night wasn't about touch. It was about recognition. A gentle acknowledgment that we had both survived something and somehow found each other on the other side.

"I'd like to do this again," I said quietly. She looked at me for a long moment, then smiled. "We will," she said. "Tonight."

That night felt magical. I was awestruck by the way she moved, graceful, grounded, completely in the moment. She didn't try to impress me. She didn't need to. Her presence alone spoke volumes. We ended the evening with a brief embrace, soft and sincere. And then I made my 200-foot pilgrimage back across the street.

It felt longer than before, like I was carrying something precious inside me now. I stayed up for hours, lying in bed, replaying every detail. Her voice. Her questions. The way she looked at me was as if I were someone worth understanding. But I couldn't quiet the questions in my head: *Could this feeling be real? Was I just caught in the glow of a rebound?* And then it happened. I sat down. And I wrote.

The words poured out of me like rivers, like lakes, like shallow, man-made ponds overflowing with impossible, blue water. I hadn't felt that in years. That pull. That rhythm. That *knowing*. For a long time, I had lost my ability to write. Some people call it writer's block, but for me, it felt like losing a best friend. A best friend so real, I gave him a name. **Genesis.**

I know he wasn't a person. Not exactly. He was a presence, a spiritual companion who had been with me through the most intimate parts of my creative life. He whispered to me in crowded rooms. He steadied me during turbulence. He comforted me in quiet spaces where God felt far away. I always believed Genesis was my connection to something divine.

Because writing has never been just a skill for me. It's my voice. It's my truest expression. It's my covenant with God. And when that voice disappeared... I felt abandoned. Not just by the words, but by the very thing that made me. At first, I thought it was writer's block. But I've come to understand it was something deeper. It was an *alignment issue*, a spiritual breach in the contract I'd signed with the gift I was given.

Because I believe this gift, this ability to write, to feel, to translate soul into language, comes with conditions. My life must remain in alignment with the spirit of the man I claimed to be. My gift doesn't operate inside the ego. It lives within grace.

When I got married, I believe I violated that alignment. I was living in a way that no longer matched the integrity of the avatar I had once created, the version of me that was rooted in truth, not performance. And so, my gift withdrew. Not out of punishment, but protection.

I believe God pulled his voice from me to protect me from my own choices. The silence was not a punishment;

it was a signal. A divine pause. And now... here we are. On this unexpected, unprecedented path. She didn't just walk into my life; she unlocked something sacred.

My voice has returned. And now, it's speaking again, whispering not just through me, but *to* me, and to the soul of a woman who, without even knowing it, has rescued me from myself.

This moment now feels like the last breath before love enters the room.

CHAPTER 2

Before We Knew What We Were

A long time ago, my father warned me about the hypnotic pull of a woman. He said they were strange, beautiful creatures, capable of bending reality into a curved, dream-like fantasy. Everything about them, he told me, was enchanting. The way they smelled. The way they moved. The clever phrasing of their words. And their rare ability to be sensual without ever being overtly sexual.

I suppose what he was saying was, *Don't fall too easily*. Don't lose yourself. Don't let love intoxicate you. But that's easier said than done. My father was a very good-looking man, and women fell for him like warm rain on southern soil. He and I are the same in some ways, but in others, we couldn't be more different.

He never knew the empowering feeling that love brings. Never stood in awe of a woman's mystique. He never fell. Not even for my mother. But I believe things might've been different if she hadn't taken her own life at just nineteen. Losing her left a silence in our house that never quite lifted, and not having a woman in the home had a profound effect on me. Still, we made the best of it.

My aunt Agnes stepped in; she was graceful, brilliant, and passionate. She understood me in ways that felt maternal, as though I were her child. She taught me etiquette, but more than that, she taught me reverence. She used books to shape my perspective on women, their strength, depth, and complexities.

I remember the summer she insisted we read 125 books about women. She didn't just want me to understand women; she wanted me to honor them. To approach them with intellect and intention. To treat them not as mysteries to solve, but as worlds to explore.

My father and Aunt Agnes were often at odds. His ideology rarely aligned with hers. He believed a man's worth was tied to what he achieved. Those emotions were distractions. He didn't think I should be with *anyone* until I had achieved my goals.

But my aunt believed I was *already* someone, and that whoever I became should treat others, especially women, accordingly. Strangely enough, I think my father would have liked the woman I'm with now. She reminds me of him in ways. Her logic. Her clarity. Her sharp edges. She thinks like him. But she *loves* differently. She loves with an intensity that I've never seen before.

Over time, what began as a single date stretched across weeks, then months, and then years. The days started to coalesce into something soft and steady. Something sacred.

Most often, the sun seemed to bless us with picture-perfect days, gentle light, soft clouds, and skies that looked like watercolor paintings. We bathed in the beauty of love. That feeling. That raw, uncut emotion. It moved through us like music. Yes, love has its mechanics, its choices, its compromises, its daily decisions. But the *art* of love... The art is spontaneous. It is spectacular.

※ ※ ※

It was a Sunday morning. The kind morning that didn't ask anything of us. No alarms. No calls. Just light, soft and golden, spilling through the curtains like it was trying not to wake us.

She was still asleep beside me, one hand resting gently against my chest, her breath rising and falling in a rhythm that made time feel slower. I didn't move. I didn't want to. There was something sacred about the weight of that moment. Something I didn't want to disturb.

I watched her for a while. Not in a way that felt intrusive, but somewhat reverent, as if I were witnessing something holy. The curve of her cheek. The way her hair spilled across the pillow. The faint crease between her brows deepened whenever she dreamed. I reached for her hand, not to hold it, but to feel it. Skin to skin.

She stirred slightly, then nestled closer, eyes still closed. Her body fit into mine like a sentence reaching its final punctuation. Not perfect. Just... right. There was no music playing. No candles lit. No romance orchestrated. But it was romantic.

In the stillness, I found something I hadn't felt in years: peace. Not just the absence of noise, but the presence of calm. Of home. Of her. When she finally opened her eyes, she didn't speak. She just looked at me, soft, a little sleepy, with that half-smile she gave when the world was still waking up. "You, okay?" she whispered. I nodded. "Yeah."

Her hand traced slow circles against my ribs, and I felt everything inside me still as if love had folded the entire world into this room, this bed, this breath between us. No grand speeches. No declarations. Just the quiet intimacy of knowing you are exactly where you're meant to be.

As she slept, my thoughts railed out of control. I wandered back to our very first dinner date. It haunts me, like a memory that refused to soften. I couldn't stop replaying it, her voice, her questions, the way her eyes seemed to look through me, not past me. There was something surgical about her presence, sharp, precise. She moved with the confidence of someone who had seen life from both the heavens and the ruins and survived them both.

I remembered the way she sat across from me, chin tilted just slightly forward, her back straight, her expression unreadable. And then she spoke, not with flirtation, but with fearless clarity.

She asked:

> *"What are you looking for?"*
>
> *"Do you need someone to talk to?"*
>
> *"Someone to hang out with?"*

And finally, with the grace of a woman who knows her worth, she said, "If you're looking for a friend, I have friends. I don't need another."

Each question hit me like a tidal wave, unexpected and unrelenting. And there I was, trying to gather my thoughts while my heart was already galloping toward something I couldn't define.

I don't even remember what I said in response. I don't think it mattered. Because even as her words worked their way through the walls of my mind, I was distracted by something entirely different: her mouth.

Yes, her mouth. Not in the way of lust, not entirely. But in the way her lips moved with elegance, the way they curved around each syllable, or how they parted gently as she took a bite. I sat there pretending to listen, but what I was doing was *memorizing*. The bend of her lips. The way she held her glass. The soft, deliberate touch of her fingers against the edge of her fork. Her every motion wrote poetry in the air.

She made femininity a language I had never fully learned. And I, once so sure of my words, was speechless. I wasn't just drawn to her. I was undone by her. And in that moment, somewhere between my silence and her certainty, I knew something had shifted. She didn't just ask questions. She set terms. She didn't just arrive. She *appeared*. And I, for all my titles and histories, was quietly falling, wondering if a man could ever be ready for a woman like Lucy.

Unfortunately, life has a way of testing your resolve the moment your heart starts to believe in peace again. My ex-wife had become increasingly volatile. Our divorce, grueling and exhausting, had left both of us scarred and battle-weary. By the time we reached any form of communication, our words were no longer bridges, but battlegrounds.

At times, I wished I could vanish, disappear from the tension, the drama, the push and pull of a past that refused to loosen its grip. But I couldn't. We shared a daughter. A beautiful little girl with health challenges that required both of her parents to be whole, even when we weren't.

In the spirit of transparency, I told my ex about Lucy. I wasn't trying to provoke her; I didn't want to live a lie. But I was blindsided by the intensity of her reaction. She was furious. Not because she wanted me, I realized. But because she didn't want *anyone else* to have me.

The weight of her anger didn't fall on me alone; it seeped into the one place she knew I would feel it the most: my relationship with my daughter. She didn't need to say much. Just enough to fray the edges of my peace. It wasn't about co-parenting. It was about control. And Lucy, without knowing it, had become the target.

Stress became my second skin. The kind that soaks through your bones and settles in your spirit. I tried to hold it all together, but it was unraveling. My mind wrestled with impossible thoughts, moments where I considered walking away to protect my daughter from the crossfire. But I couldn't. Not again. This time, I was determined to be the father I had once failed to be. The kind of parent that my dad was to me.

But stress is a silent predator. It waits, it circles, and then it strikes. I suffered two accidents at work. Small, but telling. The kind that speaks louder than you admit. The kind that costs you your career. I lost my position. And with it, I lost the fire that had once defined me as a captain. And then, like she had so many times before, Lucy crossed the street. Without drama. Without question.

Without pause. She took one look at me and said, "You can't stay here. I see what this place is doing to you."

I looked around, at the house, the memories, the weight of everything I couldn't fix. "Where would I go?" I asked. "I just lost my job. I can't afford to start over." She didn't blink. "You're coming with me," she said. "I have us. I just need *you* to take care of *yourself*."

The very next day, we packed what mattered and left the rest behind. I moved in with Lucy, and the day after that, I was working again. Because she didn't just love me, she *fought* for me. Without hesitation. Without conditions. Without needing me to be whole before she opened her arms, and in that moment, I knew I had crossed into something rare. Something sacred. A kind of love that doesn't rescue you *from* yourself...It *rescues you back* to yourself.

I wish I could tell you that once I moved across the street, everything was easy, that love wrapped us in silk and carried us toward bliss. But that wouldn't be honest.

What we found wasn't easy. It was *real*. The real that comes when two fully formed lives begin to intertwine. We were both used to leading, both born with fierce wills and strong minds. We were, in many ways, mirrors, an alpha male and an alpha female learning to dance without stepping on each other's toes. There were moments of friction, of course. But underneath it all... something softer pulsed. Something patient. Something is pulling us gently toward surrender.

I didn't mean to fall in love. Not so soon. Not so deeply. After what I had been through, I wasn't sure I believed in love anymore, at least not in the way I once did. But Lucy made believing feel possible again. There was a moment when the feeling overwhelmed me, when the words *I love you* built a cathedral in my chest and begged to be spoken.

I planned everything. Took her to dinner. Thought I'd say it over drinks, let the low lights and slow jazz create the perfect opening. But the moment passed. *Plan B*: I'd tell her in bed, in the stillness where truth is most intimate. But again, the words refused to come. I didn't have a *Plan C*. I didn't need one. She walked into the room, kissed me full on the lips, and said, with a smirk only she could deliver, "You are such a punk ass." "You've been trying to tell me you love me." "Well, I'll say it for you... *I love you.*"

That's how we were. Honest. Blunt. Soft in the middle, hard on the edges. More than anything, we were friends. Deep friends. Laugh-until-you-cry, argue-then-laugh-again, *ride-or-die* kind of friends. Before, we knew what we were. Somehow, you were already there... still.

CHAPTER 3

The Fracture

When I was in school, I wrote a paper about the nutritional value of an orange. I know, it might sound strange. But bear with me.

Growing up in Louisiana, I loved eating oranges. We had an incredible orange tree in our backyard. It wasn't just a tree; it was a teacher. Every year, I watched it grow, change, and mature with the seasons. Sometimes, I'd get eager and pick the fruit too early. The taste would hit my tongue with a sharp sourness that would curl my lips. Other times, I'd wait too long. The fruit would turn bitter, overripe, almost bad, a stomachache hidden inside citrus skin.

But when I got it just right, when the timing was perfect, the orange would burst with sweetness. Juicy, radiant, alive. It would electrify my body, give me a rush of energy, and leave me feeling full in all the right ways.

That paper I wrote wasn't just about nutrition. It was a metaphor. A quiet theory I had about men, about relationships, about life. I believed, and still believe, that people, like oranges, ripen in their own time. You can meet the right person at the wrong time, and it will feel all wrong. Sour. Or you can meet them after too much has passed, and what once held promise now carries regret. But when you meet someone at just the right moment... something extraordinary happens.

The sweetness, the balance, the nourishment, it's all there. Love, like fruit, has a season. A man, to truly love, must be ripe with experience, grounded in self-awareness, and softened by the sun of a few harsh years. He must be ready, not just to taste love, but to hold it. To appreciate the miracle of it.

Choosing someone to walk beside you is one of life's most sacred decisions. And just like that, orange, picking too soon or too late can turn something beautiful into something bitter. But when it's right... when it's just right... It feeds more than your heart. It becomes the very thing that builds you.

※ ※ ※

Fifteen years ago, I didn't understand the rules of love or even that relationships needed rules. I was naïve. If anyone had asked, my judgment should have been questioned. But no one did. And just like that, the string began to unravel.

Lucy and I seemed perfect. We did everything together, traveled, worshipped, and spent Sundays wrapped in family. We hunted for hidden treasures at flea markets and dollar stores. She introduced me to a world I never knew I needed. I was a riverboat captain. She worked in medicine.

On paper, we didn't make sense. But wandering those aisles together, laughing, searching, and surrendering to small joys, became part of our story. Our kind of joy.

We had our quirks. Our music tastes couldn't have been further apart. She'd blast that Louisiana swamp pop like it was gospel. I'd roll my eyes and laugh, quietly counting the seconds until I could slip in some rock-pop when she wasn't around. But it was those mismatches, the compromises, the soft surrender of ego, that stitched us together. Those quiet gestures said, 'I choose you anyway.'

But even as things felt right, something vital was missing. When I stepped into Lucy's world, I did just that: I stepped in. I never brought her into mine. I never unpacked the parts of me that truly mattered. I left my creative soul at the door. I hid who I was. I cloaked myself in jokes and easygoing smiles, disguising a deep truth: I was betraying my own nature. It wasn't her fault. It was mine.

Somewhere along the way, I forgot that being a captain wasn't who I was; it was just the job I did. The man behind the title? He was a writer who had simply lost his way.

And I was also a father, one who had been pushed into an impossible situation that changed the course of his daughter's life.

※ ※ ※

I still remember the day I left. My daughter, Mya, stood at the window, pounding her little hands against the glass, screaming for her dad. I watched as her mother pulled her away. She wasn't my daughter by blood, but she was my daughter. She called me "Daddy." I had tucked her in, wiped her tears, kissed her scraped knees. And I walked away. Not because I wanted to. But because I had no choice.

There's a memory I hold close, one that never fades. It was a December night, the time of year when grief lives quietly in the walls. My father had passed away years earlier in December. Every December, the weight of losing him came back with a vengeance. I would often fall into depression. One night, I couldn't sleep. I sat alone on the couch, the house silent around me. And then, out of the shadows, came Mya. Everyone else was asleep, but she saw my pain. She crawled up beside me and whispered, "I know you miss your dad... but you're my dad. And I don't like seeing you sad. I love you."

How do you make peace with losing that kind of love? How do you breathe through that kind of ache?

I know what it feels like to watch your wife fall deeper in love with a man who isn't you. I know what it means to believe in someone so deeply, only to realize you were never her choice. Not truly. Not in the way that mattered. She never crushed me with betrayal... she crushed me with comparison. With silence. With the way her eyes lit up when she talked about him. Not me.

She once said she used to marvel at the way he thought. I knew, without question, if he had asked, she would've left, and still, I smiled. I stayed. And Lucy never knew the losses I was carrying. She never knew the shattered pieces I swept into corners of myself just to seem whole. But grief has weight. It will wear you down. And eventually, you stop seeing yourself. You become a mosaic of fragments—a man made of sharp edges and soft lies.

On the outside, I looked okay. But inside, I was unraveling. I was nothing. There's a particular kind of emptiness that comes not from being abandoned, but from abandoning yourself.

It wasn't the failed marriage or the lost title that broke me. It was waking up each morning and not recognizing the man I had become. I had traded my voice for peace, my calling for companionship, my purpose for the illusion of stability. And in doing so, I had hollowed myself out in slow, imperceptible ways.

I moved through days like a ghost, performing, pretending, participating, smiling with my mouth and aching with my spirit. People saw the uniform, the charm, the strength. But they didn't see the grief I carried, the self I mourned, the dreams I quietly buried beneath the floorboards of my own home.

Now and then, something would trigger the old me. A song. A phrase. A scent. And I'd feel it, that longing, that burn. But I'd swallow it down like a man starving in public, pretending he wasn't hungry.

I had convinced myself that if I could just be "good" enough, if I could provide, protect, perform, then love would reward me. But love, real love, doesn't come to men who disappear. It comes to men who stand in their truth. And the hardest truth I had to face was this: I had vanished.

Not all at once. But slowly. Thought by thought. Compromise by compromise. Until the man I was, the writer, the dreamer, the believer, was reduced to a title, a paycheck, a shadow of someone I used to know, and in those quiet moments, when the house went still and the lights dimmed, I would sit alone in the middle of all I had built and I would whisper, "Come back." To myself. To God. To the gift. To the boy who once believed words could change the world. I missed him. I missed myself, and more than anything, I missed the *why*.

The why that came with answers I wasn't sure I wanted. The kind that burns beneath the skin and haunts the quiet hours. I had questions, questions I never dared speak aloud.

Not because the answers were hard to find, but because they were too easy to see, and deep down, I wasn't ready to face a truth I already knew. Right now, in this present moment, I can give the best version of myself, but I wasn't always like this.

※ ※ ※

When I first met Lucy, I didn't give her all of me. I gave her fragments, some bruised, some guarded. But she held them anyway. She held me, as if even my broken pieces were worth protecting, and for that, I am eternally grateful. But when a man is broken, everyone around him bleeds. Lucy was no exception. She carried the weight of my wounds, often without knowing where the bruises ended or began.

The pressure from my ex-wife never stopped. Then, one night, like fate throwing salt in healing wounds, a text arrived.

Our daughter, Tia, had fallen. Her front teeth were gone. I hadn't spoken to my ex in over a year. The silence between us had grown tall and sharp like barbed wire. When I showed Lucy the message, she tensed immediately. Her instincts flared. "It's a setup," she said. And maybe she was right. But that wasn't the point. Tia was my child, and I had to go.

Even if I was walking straight into a trap. Even if my heart was torn in two directions. Lucy didn't have children of her own. She couldn't fully understand what it meant to *have to love,* even when that love came with scars. I don't blame her. Had the roles been reversed, I might have reacted the same.

For over a year, we had picked Tia up from daycare without exchanging a single word with her mother. That was her choice. Cold. Final. And still, every time I strapped Tia into her car seat, I felt the heavy cost of peace.

According to the court, Tia was ours, half of the time. But love doesn't divide itself into percentages. It doesn't wait patiently while you work 84 hours a week to stay afloat. It doesn't understand fear, or exhaustion, or the trembling that lives in a man's hands when he's guiding a vessel, but drowning inside.

I was new to captaining, and like every other captain in their first years, I lived in fear. Fear of mistakes. Fear of sinking. Fear of being found out. But I knew this: my family needed Captain Charles. The financial responsibility alone was crushing. I set the bar so high, I almost believed I could carry it. But Captain Charles wasn't born in a vacuum. He was made possible by a friend, Maire.

The only one who knew I couldn't swim before I took the helm. She believed in me before I believed in myself. She and her family reminded me what it felt like to be *seen* without condition. To be lifted, not because of what I had done, but because of who I could become. And yet, even with love, belief, and a title... life kept carving me up.

There were no awards for being a good ex-husband. No medals for fatherhood. Just invisible bruises and sleepless nights. I had Lucy. But I wasn't equipped for the pressure that came next. She was the kind of woman you marry straight out of college, when hope still tastes like spring and the future feels manageable. But that wasn't our story.

Lucy didn't get the best of me. She inherited what remained. Looking back now, I know I didn't give myself time to heal. I ran headlong into love while I was still bleeding, and no matter how warm her embrace, my pain seeped into everything.

I don't regret loving her. I regret not understanding *what* I had in her. Eventually, the demons I'd never named began to whisper. They carved cracks in the foundation of what we'd built. Disagreements turned into distance. Patience eroded into resentment. Pride took the wheel. I refused to compromise, refused to yield. She loved me with everything she had, and I failed us.

The sun set on us slowly, and then the nightmare began. It didn't happen all at once. Love rarely dies in a storm. It fades in silence, in the soft erosion of what once felt unbreakable. I began to notice the change in quiet moments. The pauses between our conversations grew longer. The laughter we once tossed back and forth like children on a playground. It stopped showing up.

We still touched, but it was different, more out of habit than hunger. She'd reach for me in the morning, but it felt like a question. I'd hold her at night, but sometimes I wasn't there. We were both still trying...But trying isn't always enough. There were days when she would look at me with this aching in her eyes, as if she were searching for the man she met on that first date. The one who stood stunned by her beauty, who got nervous over dinner, who couldn't believe his luck. And I, I was right there next to her... But some part of me was already slipping through the cracks.

We fought more. Not over anything catastrophic, just little things. Dishes in the sink. What station was on the radio? How we spoke to each other in front of friends. But it wasn't about dishes or music. It was about everything underneath—all the unspoken fears. The weight I carried but refused to share. The emotional debts I never paid back.

She wanted to help, but I wouldn't let her. She'd say, "Talk to me." And I'd nod, lie, and say I was fine. Even when I wasn't. Especially when I wasn't. She could feel the distance, and the more she reached for me, the more

I recoiled into myself. I wanted to shield her from the darker aspects of myself. The parts are still grieving the life I'd lost. The daughter I missed. The version of myself I couldn't get back. But in trying to protect her, I shut her out.

And love, no matter how pure, can't survive behind locked doors. There was a night that I remember with painful clarity. We were sitting on the couch, a movie playing in the background, but neither of us was watching. She turned to me, her eyes soft but tired, and asked, "Are you still in this?" I didn't answer. Not because I didn't love her. But because I didn't know how to say, *I'm here... but I don't know how to stay whole.*

That silence between us that night was the moment the unraveling became real. She stopped asking after that, and we stopped offering. We moved through our days like actors hitting marks, smiling at the right cues, touching at the right beats. But the script had changed, and neither of us could find the next line. I think a part of her started grieving me before I ever left, and I, in my foolishness, let her. It wasn't that we stopped loving each other; we just stopped being heard, and that's how love often ends, not with betrayal, but with the ache of being unseen, in the same room with the person you once called home.

The separation didn't arrive with a grand announcement. No slammed doors. No suitcase on the porch. Just a quiet unraveling that had already been happening for months. It began with the little things. We stopped waiting for each other to eat. Stopped checking in during the day. Stopped lingering in the hallway just to steal a kiss. The distance settled in. I loved her too much to ask her to keep doing it. I remember the night that everything finally broke. "*The fracture*"

CHAPTER 4

After the Fire, Before the Light

There is a silence that comes after the burn. Not the kind that soothes or comforts, but the kind that settles in the chest like a weight, a hush where love once bloomed and laughter once echoed. It's the silence of things unsaid, and the aftermath of a goodbye that never properly arrived.

Time moved forward, as it always does, carrying me with it like driftwood down a river of new beginnings. I tried to let her go. I tried to forget the sound of her voice, the way it cracked softly when she said "I love you," like something sacred being released into the world. But that whisper stayed with me.

It haunted the quiet moments. It curled around my thoughts when the world grew still. It was not memory. It was an echo. Years passed. We reunited, briefly. But time, like love, is delicate in its arrangement. We fought. She walked away, and this time, she didn't come back. She blocked my number, and just like that, the thread between us snapped.

In my heart, I knew the door was still there. I could've gone to her. Knocked. Pleaded. Fallen to my knees if need be. All she wanted, all she ever needed, was to know she was worth the effort. But I didn't go. I didn't knock. I didn't beg. Because something in me couldn't bow.

I had been raised by a father made of logic and silence, a 20-year military man who believed emotion was a liability. He taught me how to survive storms, not how to mend what storms broke. His lessons were clear: Don't cry. Don't chase. Don't break. Just endure. If your heart is shattered in January, by December, you'll forget the shape of the pain.

It was foolish. But it was the only blueprint I had. Without a mother, I missed the softer curriculum of love, learning how to nurture, yield, and return. In that gap, I failed Lucy. She needed tenderness. What I gave was endurance.

As much as I loved her, I let her go. Not with grace. Not with closure. Just... absence. No goodbye. No final embrace. Only silence where promises once lived. A memory of what might have been, left behind like an unopened letter in a rainstorm, and in that quiet, the sun began to set inside me. The warmth slipped away, and the dark, not empty, but full of consequence, rose with retribution in its vocabulary, and regret in every syllable.

As the years passed, life settled into something quieter, less like a storm, more like a steady tide. I became engulfed in the rhythms of fatherhood. Everywhere I went, it was me and Tia. She became my reason, my ritual, my reset. She didn't just give me purpose, she gave me a place to pour all the love I still carried but didn't know where to put, and maybe, in some unconscious way, she saved me.

Dating became nearly impossible, not because I didn't want companionship, but because nothing and no one could compare to the role I had stepped into. I had committed to being a father first, and every other identity came second.

Over time, the once-hostile dynamic between my ex-wife and me softened into something resembling a peaceful relationship. She once told me, "Watching you with Tia made me miss you." She said she loved seeing how I parented.

Maybe it stirred something in her, nostalgia, regret, or just the comfort of knowing I turned out to be who I said I'd be, and sure, maybe the child support checks helped smooth the edges. I'm joking. Kind of...

Still, there was mutual respect between us. We couldn't make the relationship last, but it hadn't all been a lie. It was real for me. Painfully real. But no matter what I gave, no matter how hard I tried, there was always a shadow hanging over us. Him.

That man. Her first love. Her blueprint. I could never scrub him from my mind. He lived there, like an echo I never invited in, and try as I might, I couldn't compete with the ghost of her desire.

I closed my eyes, and there they were, entwined, lost in each other, immersed in the kind of hunger I wanted for myself. The jealousy, the shame, the images I couldn't unsee, they haunted me longer than I care to admit. I was angry for years, angry at her, at him, at myself. But woven into that anger was something deeper: grief.

Because even while my mind replayed that betrayal, my heart was still caught somewhere else, caught in the memory of the one woman I believed would never betray me. Lucy. And the hardest truth I had to face? She was gone. Not just physical, but gone from the narrative, gone from the possibility of us, and I had no one to blame but time, and the version of me that didn't fight hard enough to keep her.

※ ※ ※

In time, I met other women, each remarkable in their own right. There was Bri. A chocolate goddess, sultry in every step. Her voice carried sex appeal in every syllable, spilling warmth with each breath she released.

She worked for the IRS but moved like a muse from another realm, sending daily photos of herself wrapped in fabrics that dazzled the mind. She was exotic. Electric. But desire alone is not enough to build a life. One argument was all it took. The long flights. The mismatched timing.

Like so many things in my life then, it ended just as quickly as it began. So, I returned to what I knew. The pen. The boats. Work, work, and more work. I buried myself in the familiar. A year later, Malina entered my life—a woman with soft eyes and a soft heart, Hispanic, with a twist of Louisiana soul.

We met on Facebook, drawn together by timing and a shared need for something new. She had been broken. I had been busy pretending not to be.

She was intrigued by my writing, by my fire, by my wounds, and for a while, her tenderness became a bomb.

But healing can't be borrowed, and love can't be sustained when half of your heart still lives in the past. Eventually, she returned to the man she had tried to forget. He looked like me. Came from the same place. But he wasn't me, and yet, I couldn't blame her.

She needed closure, and I... I needed clarity. I don't regret Malina. She reminded me that I could still feel, even when I thought I was numb. Even in that loss, I gained something; I gained myself.

I'm not telling you about these women to diminish them. Each one added something to my story, each one a chapter I needed to write through and walk through. They were blessings, unexpected and unfinished. But I was still running from my truth.

God had begun whispering. Not loud or dramatic. Soft. Constant. Insistent. After Malina, I returned home. To heal. To write. To unravel. I was condensed into something small, something unrecognizable.

※ ※ ※

The walls around me closed in, yet strangely, I didn't resist. There was pain, but also space. A void, yes, but a sacred one. It's hard to explain what it means to write in total submission to God and nature.

It's like being dismantled by the silence, then remade by it. The Mississippi River became my confessional. The boats, my cathedral, and at night, the only sound was the echo of heartbreak mingling with the weight of history.

I had begun writing a story that wasn't just mine. It was theirs. The ancestors. The forgotten. The enslaved. And with every keystroke, my pain folded into theirs. This wasn't writing. It was a sacrifice. It was devotion. My tears fell not just for lost love, but for stolen legacies, for lives buried without names, for voices that could only be resurrected through ink and blood.

In that chamber of isolation, I stopped writing *about* my pain and started writing *through* it.

However, the loneliness that comes with isolation can feel like a storm with no eye, a silence so loud it rattles the soul. So, I revisited the idea of Lucy. I never stopped believing that she still carried love for me, even if that love was buried somewhere in the shadows of all we lost.

As fate would have it, her town had been ravaged by a hurricane. The winds had torn through streets and memories alike. Maybe, I thought, this was my moment, not to rescue her, but to return with humility. To rebuild more than just wood and brick. Maybe this was divine timing.

I drove to her house, half-expecting the door to open and reveal some towering bodybuilder in my place. A man who had stepped in while I had walked away. But when I knocked, the sound echoed back like a memory. No one answered. The house was empty.

Still, I wasn't deterred. For once, I laid my pride down at the altar of what might still be possible. I drove across town to her mother's house, unsure of what I would say or how I would be received. I knocked again; this time, the knock didn't echo. The door opened, and there she was. Lucy. As beautiful and fierce as ever. The years hadn't dulled her glow; they had sharpened it. She stood there like a dream I had no right to revisit, and yet... she didn't close the door.

I stammered a hello, my voice catching in my throat. I told her I'd help her rebuild, that she could come to stay with me.

She refused, and I expected as much. But the moment was sacred. Two souls, two feet apart, yet somehow still entirely worlds away. Later that evening, we had dinner. It was less reunion and more reckoning. She grilled me, not out of bitterness, but from a place that once believed in forever. She asked the hard questions. She reminded me of how I left.

She said she couldn't go back down that road again, and I understood. For once, I didn't argue with fate. I didn't fight for what I had failed to protect.

I walked away again, this time knowing exactly what I was losing. I returned to the quiet company of pen and pad. But now, the page wasn't empty. It held the weight of what I couldn't keep. The grief of loving too late. You never know the path God has written for you.

Some of us love in chapters. Some lose their soulmates while still alive. Some of us write not for applause or approval, but to survive.

Writers write. Singers sing. Dancer's dance. Not because they are told to, but because their spirit cannot do otherwise.

※ ※ ※

Two years had passed since I last heard Lucy's voice. Time had done what time always does: it softened the edges, blurred the memory, but never quite erased it.

Then one day, out of the blue, my friend Calvin called. He said he'd been trying to reach me. He said, "Man, it's time," he told me. "You need to start dating again." Normally, I would've brushed him off, offered a polite laugh, and gone back to my books and my boats. But something was different this time. Maybe it was the quiet in my house. Maybe it was the ache that had stopped screaming but still throbbed in silence.

His wife had someone in mind. "She's nice," she said. "Smart. Grounded. Been through some things, but she's a good woman." I trusted her judgment. Still, I hesitated. How could I not? It's hard to move on with someone else when you're in love with your soulmate.

My mind wandered, uninvited, thinking about Lucy. We weren't getting back together. I had tried. Lord knows I had tried. I don't even know what I expected from her anymore, mercy? Closure? A second chance? I just wish I'd told her the truth while I had the chance.

I wanted forever. I wanted her to wear my ring, to share my name, the name my father gave me, the name I try to honor every day.

But I didn't say it. I didn't say anything, and silence has a way of writing endings all by itself. So, I gave in. I told Calvin to pass along my number, and within minutes, she called. She said My name is Karen. She moved at the speed of bliss, soft-spoken and poised. She had the kind of voice that felt practiced for podiums and peacekeeping.

She said all the right things, but it wasn't just her tone; it was her story. Her struggle. Her rise from the ashes felt eerily familiar.

She had been married twice, both endings loud and unforgiving. I asked her, "What's the one thing your ex-husbands would complain about?" She didn't flinch. "They said I got a cold. Distant."

At the time, I didn't think too much of it. We were just starting. But looking back now…I should have listened a little deeper.

※ ※ ※

Karen once told me that her mother suffered from mental illness. She said that they moved often, drifting between California and Louisiana like a leaf caught in someone else's storm. Because of her condition, her mom couldn't work. So, Karen and her sister did what they could, small jobs, long hours, just to keep the lights on.

When they were kids, they didn't have a bed. They slept under a table. Four children growing up in the shadows of instability.

One brother, gentle but a little slow. One sister, strung out on drugs but generous to a fault, the kind of woman who would give you her last breath if you asked. And then there was the other sister, a force of nature. She graduated from Penn State, the kind of woman who made resilience look effortless.

Karen grew up in California. When she was sixteen, she came home from school one day to find the house empty. Her mother had vanished.

She never told me what happened after that, and I never asked. But I wish I had. I wish I'd asked the questions that make you uncomfortable. The questions that make you understand.

I remember one night in particular. We had gone to dinner, small talk, laughter, something electric in the air. Afterward, she asked if I wanted to see where she lived.

The first time I stepped into Karen's home, she asked me to spend the night. We sat in her bedroom, watching television, and then, without hesitation, she kissed me. Something came over me.

I gently pushed her away, not out of rejection but confusion. She looked at me, lips parted, eyes burning with certainty. "You figured it out," she said. "Figured what out?" "That you're going to marry me."

God. She said out loud what I was thinking in silence. What the hell was happening? I stood up, stunned. "I should go," I said. "But I want you to stay," she whispered. "We can go to the store, get you some clothes."

I left. But part of me believed, still believes, that God was trying to tell me something. That night stayed with me. That was then. But now... I wonder if I was drugged at dinner. I can't prove it, but the feeling never quite left.

Despite everything, we spent more and more time together. She would cook for me, but the food had no smell, and I never once saw her eat. I don't know what came over me, but within months, I proposed.

The moment was thrilling. Surreal and strange. But looking back, it lacked something critical. Truth. It wasn't long before the truth came crashing in. It's the moment when illusion meets reality, and you're caught between what you hoped for and what you now know.

We had decided that I would propose at a restaurant in New Orleans. I wish I could remember the name, but the image remains etched in my mind, dim candlelight, soft music, and a view that looked like the sun had poured its gold into the sky just for us. It felt like a scene written by fate. Until it wasn't. That night marked the first time I saw the real person peek out from behind the carefully constructed persona.

We had over sixty guests. Family, friends, coworkers, people from different chapters of our lives, all gathered at one table. My brother was there. My daughter, radiant with joy. My sister. Even my first ex-wife. Karen had insisted on inviting her as an attempt to show unity. But the energy was... off. Thick. Awkward.

When I rose from my seat and reached into my pocket for the ring, the room fell silent. You could feel the collective breath being held, and then I saw it.

Karen took a deep gulp of her drink. Not a sip. Not a toast. A full-bodied, nerves-fraying swallow. I noticed it, but told myself she was just nervous. This was a big moment. I gave her the benefit of the doubt.

We went through the motions. The applause. Congratulations. She smiled, but it felt rehearsed.

Her friend, Lanika, had been sitting at another table. Karen kept looking over at her, distracted. Then, without warning, she rushed across the room.

I was shaking hands, receiving well-wishes, when Karen suddenly reappeared, storming up to me, eyes wild, voice sharp. "Lanika is over there talking about sucking dick," she blurted out. Loud. Unfiltered. Right in front of my family. I froze.

The room spun, but not from champagne. My mouth opened, but no words came out. Just silence and secondhand shame. Her friend Demetrise approached, laughing nervously. "She's had a little too much to drink," she said, trying to smooth it over.

My friend leaned in, quiet but firm. "I don't know, Captain..." Then my brother. The one who rarely says much. He looked me dead in the eyes and said, "This isn't you. You don't like people who act like that."

He was right. Every cell in my body knew it. But I didn't leave. I didn't walk away. I convinced myself that I had to stay. That I was doing the noble thing. That I had already gone too far to turn around. I told myself I could fix it. I confused commitment with self-sacrifice.

Later that night, my brother called me. "Lucy," he said. Just her name. Then he added, "She would've been the better choice."

I didn't disagree. I just sat there with the phone in my hand, staring at a future I had already started walking into, long before I realized I'd taken the wrong path. It was too late. It was a fracture. The moment when illusion meets reality. I was committed. Until the final curtain call.

Months later, we started looking for the perfect place to get married. She was practical, suggesting an art gallery. But I was a captain. I wanted something that mirrored my status, something with history, with grandeur.

I chose a mansion on New Orleans' famed St. Charles Avenue, majestic, lavish, dripping with old Southern charm. This time, no ex-wives were allowed. The big day arrived. My daughter stood beside me as my best man. My brother was there, protective and watchful. My best friend, Rev Franklin, was the one to marry us.

Just before the ceremony, I was in a quiet room away from the music, the guests, and the cameras. A videographer was mic'ing me up when my brother leaned in with a question I'll never forget. "Are you sure?" he asked. "I always thought it would be Lucy." "But if this is what you want, I'm okay with it." I didn't have an answer. Not a real one. But we went through with it.

By the time the vows were exchanged, the signs were already there. Karen had begun pulling me away from friends, quit her job, and was slowly unraveling in silence.

We came home that night as husband and wife and never touched each other again. No hugs. No kisses. No intimacy.

One day, I asked her about it, about us, and she looked me in the eyes and said:

> *"If you need sex, maybe you should get yourself a fucking whore."*

That was our beginning. A month later, we went to brunch, our first outing as a married couple, and there she was. Lucy.

She walked in with a man beside her. Muscle-bound. Rough around the edges. But he was just a shadow standing next to her light. I turned and whispered to Karen, "Oh shit... that's Lucy."

To my surprise, Karen wanted to meet her. I didn't like the idea. Something about it felt dangerous. But I agreed. We walked up. I tapped Lucy on the shoulder. She turned. Her eyes met Karen's. In that instant, something passed between them. It wasn't just a look; it was a reckoning.

It was a thunderclap in silence. Karen stepped back. She looked at me and asked, "What did you do to her?" "She must hate you." But it wasn't hate. It was heartbreak dressed in quiet defiance, and in that moment, Karen knew what Lucy and I had never spoken aloud. Love doesn't always fade. But sometimes...It expires. *Even in the smoke, I searched for you... Still. After the Fire, Before the Light.*

CHAPTER 5

The Diagnosis

Three months into the marriage, I decided to schedule a long-overdue physical. I hadn't been to the doctor in over three years, but I figured I'd walk in, get my usual clean bill of health, and walk right back out. I looked good. I felt decent. I assumed I was fine. That was a fool's assumption.

You can look like a statue of health on the outside and still fall dead before lunch. But that wasn't my fate, not yet.

I'd been going to the same doctor for more than twenty years. We shared pleasantries. It felt routine. Then he asked if I wanted to do a prostate exam, and I immediately said no. Last time he checked, I walked out with more than a bruise to my pride. I told him, "No disrespect, doc, but I still remember those big fingers."

We both laughed, but something in me said I should've just let him check. Instead, he ran bloodwork.

A few hours later, the results came in. My PSA levels were high. Dangerously high. On a scale from 1 to 20, anything between 1 and 4 is normal. I was 19.5. They didn't explain much. Just referred me to a specialist.

When I arrived at the clinic, a young female doctor entered the room. She made a nervous joke about having small fingers—trying to ease the discomfort. I appreciated the humor, but I was still tense. After her examination, she said the senior physician would have to check again. And when he walked in, all I could think was, *God help me, he has big ass fingers.*

I joke, but none of this was funny. Not then. Not now. After the second examination, the doctor didn't waste time. "You have prostate cancer," he said plainly. The room shrank. My breath collapsed inward. The walls felt like they were pressing in on me, tighter with each heartbeat. I became numb. From that moment forward, everything changed.

The treatments came fast. The sickness followed faster. Within months, I was prepped for surgery. I remember the morning of the procedure, Karen woke up, looked at me, and said nothing. Not a word. Just silence. We rode to the hospital like strangers.

My brother, my daughters, Rev Franklin, and even both of my ex-wives were there, but my ex-wives didn't come into the room. Not because they didn't care, but because they didn't want to disrespect my marriage. Still, they waited the entire time.

After surgery, I lay in recovery, trying to piece myself together. King looked at me and said, softly,

> *"I don't think this marriage is going to last."*

Then my daughter leaned in and whispered,

> "Dad... I don't think she cares about you."

Their words stunned me. But deep down, I had already started to feel it. They just gave voice to what I couldn't yet admit. Karen never took time off to care for me. Not a single day.

While I lay in bed healing from a life-altering surgery, she was on the phone with her girlfriends, planning nights out. When Mardi Gras arrived in New Orleans, she was in the streets from Friday through Tuesday, dancing, drinking, living like nothing had changed.

Meanwhile, I had to fight my way to the kitchen just to cook myself a meal. No hugs. No tenderness. Just distance. And indifference.

There's one memory I'll never forget: I had a complication and had to be rushed to the emergency room. I had a bad infection, COVID, and cancer. Karen brought me there... but she didn't stay. She left me in the hospital. Left me alone, battling the scariest fight of my life. Where was the love? Where was the care? What had I done to deserve this?

The tension at home grew unbearable. Karen had emotionally checked out. She told me, flat-out, that she wanted to separate.

> "I'm so sick of hearing about cancer!" she screamed.

Those words echoed like a knife being twisted. In my weakest hour, she turned her back on me. I packed my things and moved in with Rev Franklin. After a week, he looked at me one morning and asked, quietly, "Where's Erin?" I didn't have an answer.

She was nowhere to be found, and neither, it seemed, was the woman I thought I had married. I was officially living in the Twilight Zone. *The Diagnosis...*

CHAPTER 6

When the World Went Quiet

The ring. The betrayal. The silence where presence should have been. How do you put into words what it feels like to be abandoned by your wife at the very moment you needed her the most?

I wish I could tell you it was a night. That the air was heavy, that thunder rolled low in the distance, that the sky mirrored the ache inside me. But the truth is, it wasn't like that. The weather was good. The sun rose, the breeze moved gently through the trees, and the day appeared ordinary.

But I wasn't. Inside, I was wrecked. Looking back, I can safely say this: sometimes life doesn't turn out the way you imagine. Sometimes, it doesn't storm. It doesn't howl.

It doesn't even warn you. Sometimes, the sky is clear, and you are the storm.

After staying with Rev Franklin for a few months, my phone lit up. It was a text. From Karen. *Are you okay?* I stared at the screen, unsure what to feel. Relief? Confusion? Anger?

The texts came rarely, just enough to stir something inside me, but not enough to offer any comfort. She would say a few words and then vanish again. I counted how many times she reached out. The number was so small, it's almost embarrassing to admit.

What I *can* count, though, are the times she told me she didn't need me. The times she told me she didn't need *any* man.

"Dick comes a dime a dozen," she screamed once. I still hear it.

It's hard to talk about abandonment. But with cancer, the pain of it takes on a new shape.

I remember the first time I walked into the Tom Benson Cancer Center. I was scared, not a kind of fear that rattles your nerves for a moment, but a deeper, bone-shaking terror.

The waiting room was filled with older faces. At 54, I felt like the youngest person in the room. I didn't say much. I didn't know what to say. I sat there, trapped inside my thoughts, haunted by questions I didn't have the strength to ask.

When the nurse finally called my name, I braced myself for another cold, clinical examination. But instead, the doctor sat me down. He didn't touch me. He didn't rush. He *talked* to me. For three hours. He wanted to know me, not just my charts, my numbers, my diagnosis. Me. He asked about my kids. He asked about my wife.

I told him the truth. The humiliating, uncomfortable truth, and he listened. When I was done, he shook his head softly.

> "I'm sorry," he said. "I'm sorry she isn't here. Family is vital to recovery. I can't change your wife. But I can help you."

He did help. He connected me with a psychiatrist, not just for the cancer, but for the failing marriage, and as if that wasn't enough, in the middle of everything, I broke my foot in three places. More doctors. More hospitals. More questions with no answers.

Looking back, I'm not sure how I felt. It was complicated. My life had become complicated. I started falling apart, not from the cancer itself, but from the loneliness that wrapped itself around every moment.

One doctor gave me an injection to shut down my body's testosterone. I'm not an emotional man by nature. But that shot? It opened a floodgate I couldn't close. I cried at everything. I cried at nothing. I cried because I was alone. I thought I was a strong man. I had always believed that.

But sitting in those waiting rooms, I finally understood why those older patients always had someone with them, someone to hold their hand, to whisper that it would be okay.

I didn't have that. I lost count of how many times I sat in an ER by myself, the walls closing in, monitors beeping, nurses rushing by, and all I could do was stare at the ceiling and wonder if this was how it ended.

Every time I slipped into that darkness, every time I felt the weight of death leaning in, I thought about my mother and father. I wanted them there. I wanted to hear their voices, telling me it was going to be okay.

My father would not have left me by myself, and my mother—God, I never even knew what it was like to have one. She died when I was two years old. But in those moments, I missed her like I'd known her all my life. It would have been nice.

I remember crying every night. I remember the doctor asking me after the surgery, *"Are you ready to fight for your life?"* If you had cut me open that day, you wouldn't have found courage. You wouldn't have found resolve. You would have seen despair, raw, bleeding, and wrapped in flesh.

It's so hard to deal with the idea of limited days and eternal nights, infected with the silence of death. My death. I'm not sure if it was the medical process or my failing marriage, but I was broken in the worst way.

The days after surgery blurred together. The nights were worse. Grief sat on my chest like a heavy animal, and the house was too quiet, even with Rev Franklin moving around in the next room.

I'd wake up drenched in sweat, unsure if it was the cancer, the medication, or the loneliness tearing at me.

I would stare at the ceiling, my mind full of voices that weren't there, my father's, calm and unshakable; the mother I never knew; Karen's sharp, cutting words, echoing even in her absence.

I don't remember praying at first. I just... talked. Talked to the ceiling. Talked to God. Talked to the version of myself I used to be, and somewhere in all that talking, something started whispering back.

It wasn't loud. It wasn't even comforting, not yet. But it was something. I still cried. I cried every night.

But slowly, I began to write again, not because I wanted to, but because I had to. The notebook sat on the table beside my bed, and one night, without thinking, I picked up the pen.

The words didn't come in neat sentences. They came in fragments. Scrawled, uneven thoughts. Broken prayers. But they came.

I can't tell you I felt "better." I didn't. The cancer wasn't gone. The loneliness wasn't gone. The betrayal still burned, and Erin was still gone.

But the writing, the act of moving what was inside of me onto the page, felt like opening a window in a sealed room. The air changed, even if just a little.

That's when I started to understand something I hadn't before: healing doesn't come all at once. It doesn't arrive like a trumpet blast or a sunrise. It's slower than that. It's quieter.

It comes in moments, a line of ink, a single prayer, a whispered memory of a mother you never knew. It comes in the night when you don't even know you're asking for it. That's how I survived those months. Not because I was strong. Not because I wasn't broken. But because God gave me back my voice, my voice kept me alive.

CHAPTER 7

The Ring That Wasn't a Ring

The fight wasn't over. My doctor told me I would need radiation. I had hoped, naively, that the surgery would end it, that the scalpel would cut everything away, and I'd be able to say, I survived. But that would have been too simple.

I guess losing my wife, my home, and my sense of safety wasn't enough. Maybe it was me, perhaps I wasn't a good person.

Maybe when I thought I was hearing God's voice, it wasn't him at all, just my voice bouncing back at me, reinforcing what I wanted to believe. I don't think I was a bad person.

I was an artist. Even as a captain, I still moved like an artist, defining landscapes, shaping things unseen into things you could hold. If I had committed a crime, it would've been betraying myself.

Maybe my gift, the ability to transcribe life into words, to turn pain into art, was God's will for me, and maybe I was being punished for failing to listen. But not like this. I felt like God had lost track of my soul.

The doctor explained that, even though the cancer had been cut out, it hadn't stayed put. When they opened me, they discovered my prostate had burst, spilling cancer cells into the rest of my body. I was in stage four.

I didn't have a smile to offer. All I had to give was a polite "thank you."

The nurse who had always met me with a smile stood by his side. This time, her head hung low. She didn't speak. But her silence dimmed the light in the room, as if she had reached over and blown out the last candle.

When I got up to leave, she pressed a small card into my hand. It read: God has not forgotten about you. Those words didn't comfort me. They haunted me. They made me question my questions, ask my doubts if they were justified.

If God hasn't forgotten me, why does it feel like I'm wandering this world alone?

But there were small glimmers. I saw who loved me. My friend Calvin and I had drifted apart; life and ambition, and Karen drove a wedge between us.

We hadn't spoken in over a year. Then one day, his wife texted. She told me Calvin's birthday was coming, that he loved me, and that she wanted to surprise him by having me show up.

My foot was broken. My stomach was sliced open and wired shut. But I had to go. Not because I wanted to surprise him, but because I needed family. He was my friend. My brother and I needed my brother.

That night, Calvin's band was performing. When the music stopped and the applause rose, I stood there as the lights dimmed, and Calvin saw me. He didn't say much at first. He didn't need to. He just pulled me in, and in his eyes, I saw it, the love that comes from a place deeper than the heart.

That night, I went back to Rev Franklin's house. I sat down, the weight of the day pressing on me like wet clothes, and then the phone rang.

It wasn't a wedding ring. It wasn't the ring of forever. It was the ring of a phone. But it might as well have been an earthquake.

By then, I had grown used to the silence, the kind that seeps into your bones, makes the world feel cold and empty, and then the phone rang. The Ring That Wasn't a Ring. A simple sound. But it ruptured the quiet.

I stared at the glowing screen. My name. My number. It hadn't meant much to anyone in a long time. I didn't know what to expect if I answered. Maybe nothing. Maybe something that would hurt.

But I answered, and her voice came through the line. A voice I knew better than my thoughts. A voice I thought I might never hear again.

It wasn't a wedding ring. But that sound, that voice, slipped around my heart like one. Not the promise of forever. But the reminder that some promises never stop echoing.

"Hello?" The word barely made it out of my mouth. On the other end, there was a pause, the kind of pause that stretches into forever, the kind that feels like it's holding its breath. Then came her voice. Soft. Careful. "Hi... It's me." My chest tightened.

I hadn't heard that voice in what felt like lifetimes, yet it was instantly familiar, like stumbling into an old song you'd long forgotten, only to find you still knew every word. She didn't say her name. She didn't have to. There was only one *her*. She breathed out, then in. I could almost hear her gathering herself.

I heard... I heard you were in trouble. I swallowed hard. "Yes," I said, barely above a whisper. Another pause. Her silence didn't feel empty. It felt *heavy*, like she was holding all the weight of everything we'd been and everything we weren't anymore.

"I wanted to see you," she said, and those words, just five simple words, hit me harder than the diagnosis, harder than the surgery, harder than the endless silence I'd been living in. Not because they promised anything.

But because they cracked open something inside me I thought had long ago sealed shut. I agreed to see her. But the truth? I was terrified. Terrified of what I'd look like through her eyes. Terrified of what her presence might awaken in me.

Terrified that I might not survive the sound of her walking away a second time. That night, I lay in bed staring at the ceiling, the phone still warm in my hand, her voice lingering like smoke, not the kind that chokes you, but the kind that clings to your clothes, your skin, your soul.

I thought of all the things I should have said. All the things I would say when I saw her again. But mostly, I thought about how it felt just to hear her voice, and for the first time in a very long time, I didn't feel entirely alone.

After I heard her voice, I knew that somehow, God had listened to my prayers, too. She didn't care why we broke up. She didn't want to dissect the wreckage. "All is forgiven," she whispered. "Now it's time to make you better."

Phones ring around me all the time, but never like this. The weeks that followed blurred into treatments and hospital rooms. Every day, I drank three bottles of water before my radiation treatment.

I had to time it perfectly; the water lifted my bladder so they could aim where my prostate used to be. One day, I miscalculated. I drank too much, too soon.

I climbed onto the cold table, naked, and a small towel was draped across me for dignity's sake. The machine whirred to life... and my bladder gave way. A flood.

I screamed, the nurse ran in, and suddenly there was water everywhere, on me, on her, on the table. I bolted for the restroom, naked, straight into the hallway. The nurse caught me, smiling softly. "It's okay," she said, "I understand." Her kindness only deepened my embarrassment.

Another time, I stumbled out of the radiation chamber and collapsed. A friend saw me, and after that, he never let me go alone again.

Through it all, Lucy called. Every morning before treatment. Every evening after. Her voice became the steady rhythm my body couldn't give me. Rev Franklin, too, gave me more of his time than I can ever repay. He was 80 years old.

I had nursed him through colon cancer, and he stood beside me through mine.

But even in all that pain, I knew what I wanted. I wanted her. Imagine this: I had cancer. She came to help. She said, "It's good we can hang out as friends," then added, "but I don't trust you with my heart anymore."

I couldn't help myself, I asked for another chance. She paused, then said, "You haven't asked me anything. I'm still on the market until you ask me. But we can revisit this another time."

I didn't understand women. I thought the subject was closed. But she hadn't let it go. The next day, she found a way to make me ask again, the right way.

That night, we went to Dave & Buster's. Something was different. She locked onto me in a way she hadn't before, an unending, steady gaze. At one point, she hugged me from behind, her voice trembling as she whispered, "I love you."

I turned to her, and she said it again, louder this time, as if the words had been trapped too long. "I just... love you."

I was stunned. This was the same woman who had once said, I love you as a friend only. The same woman who swore she didn't trust me with her heart. Now I know, she didn't hate me.

She hated the things I did. She hated the pieces of the man I used to be. But she didn't stop loving me.

My failed marriage forced me to see things differently. My cancer humbled me. It softened my edges, and now, when we spoke, it was harmony, not friction.

There's something to be said about love that reconnects in the worst circumstances. Love that finds you bruised and bandaged, and holds you anyway.

One night, we were lying across the bed when she told me her truth. "I waited for you to come to my door for over five years," she said softly. "All you had to do was kiss me and tell me you loved me, and I would have been yours again."

My heart cracked at her words. Shattered, then rebuilt. The ring I got wasn't a ring. It wasn't gold or silver or the promise of forever.

It was just a phone call. But that ring, the one I should have given, should have been more than a phone that rings.

It should have been the ring of something certain, the kind you don't take off.

As I lay there that night, her words and her voice still wrapped around me, I understood something for the first time: Sometimes the smallest ring, just a sound, just a voice on the line, can be louder than every silence you've ever known, and sometimes, it's not the end of a chapter. It's the *start* of one. *In the silence, my heart called your name.... Still*

CHAPTER 8

The Ring that Changed Everything

James Baldwin once said that the worst nightmare for any writer isn't rejection or obscurity, it's the endless isolation. He spoke about the way loneliness stalks an artist, and how the gift you carry feels less like a blessing and more like a burden you can't ever lay down. He said, *"As an artist, you can't tell the truth, but you have to live by the truth."*

I have spent so many nights turning those words over in my mind like stones in my hands. What did Baldwin mean? Was he warning me? Was he preparing me, or was he holding up a mirror?

For me, Baldwin's words mean this: I may never know complete happiness, and I will probably fail in the one thing that has saved my life again and again, love.

Because when I write, I speak in my voice. And in that voice, I choose freedom. But freedom has its own cost. You can't speak the truth without cutting someone, somewhere.

※ ※ ※ ※

So here we are. The cancer is gone. My soulmate has returned. I wish I could tell you that meant we slipped into the sunset, hand in hand, no shadows at our heels. But life doesn't hand out sunsets like that. Life demands its sacrifices.

Do you remember the note? The one that started this whole thing? The one that ended with five quiet words: *"He could use a friend."* That note changed everything. But did it?

Because here's the truth, I told my cousin Brandon what to write. I told him what to say because I believed my words would speak to her heart.

He became my voice that day. He delivered my words, and that truth, that carefully chosen truth, became its own kind of lie. Lucy loved that note. But she won't read my writings now. And writing... writing is my voice.

How do you love someone who refuses to hear you? How do you speak when the words that define you go unread?

I am the spaces between the lines, but right now, I feel like the mistake people always erase. She doesn't understand, and maybe I can't hold that against her.

But there's a difference between not understanding and not *wanting* to understand.

When we were together before, I didn't speak. I didn't tell her what I felt. My silence peeled away the orange before it was ripe.

Back then, the thing she hated most was that I wouldn't put my heart on the line. I stayed safe.

Now here I am, my heart bleeding out across these pages for anyone to see, and I'm being told that part of me, the part that bleeds, isn't required.

Maybe this is a test. Maybe God sent her back to rebuild the will I thought I'd lost. But I wish He would give me a sign.

I wish He would speak to me in these lines and blank spaces where I spend my life listening.

As much as I've endured, I still wonder if I'm where I belong. Because love, real love, can be romanticized, but it can also be heavy, sharp, imperfect.

When Karen kissed me for the first time, I thought God was speaking to me. Maybe I was wrong. Or maybe I just didn't understand the language He was speaking. Maybe he was leading me somewhere unfamiliar, for reasons He hadn't revealed yet.

※ ※ ※ ※

The first time I met Lucy, my head was too far in the clouds to hear her voice. Even after we broke, I was too far inside myself to humble myself enough to repair what we had.

Lucy told herself she hated me. So, when she showed up to help, I was baffled. Why would this woman reach for me if I'd hurt her the way I had?

I believe there's one person, just one, who supersedes logic, who defies reason, who exists outside the lines of ordinary love.

For my ex-wife, it was the father of her child. For me, it's Lucy. I'm the name at the bottom of that note. But even now, I wonder: which version of me was she answering? Captain Charles? Charles, the man? Or Charles Hamilton, the writer?

It's hard to hear love when you're still at war. But even in that war, I can listen to God's drums beating. His grace has brought me to my knees.

I've prayed for the mercy to let me be happy, even if happiness is only borrowed, even if it's only for a moment.

I don't know what comes next. All I know is this: I must continue to live my truth. I love Lucy, but this story isn't just about us. It's about everyone who's ever loved and lost and loved again.

I will never sacrifice my pen. I will keep telling the stories God hands me in the stillness. Because I know *Genesis*, that whisper in the blank spaces, will always speak to me.

And that note? That simple note with those quiet words? It's the glue that holds the meaning of love together. **Still.**

We are unfinished by design. Lucy is by my side. Not fully invested in the writer, but steadfast for the man. She loves me in the way she can, and maybe that's enough, maybe love is always just what we have to give, in the measure we can offer it. One day, I hope to give her a ring that doesn't ring. And me? I'm here, at this desk, writing.

The sun is lowering, brushing the sky in colors I could never mix by hand, no matter how many words I tried. The stillness before an approaching sunset is its own kind of sermon. It whispers things you can't always hear in the noise of the day.

I sit, I watch, and I write. Each keystroke feels like a prayer, not for an ending, not for answers, but for the courage to keep telling the truth, even when it hurts, even when it costs.

God is here. Not in grand gestures. Not in miracles split wide open. He's here in the small things. The sound of Lucy in the kitchen. The scratch of this pen. The hush of evening is creeping across the floor, and somewhere between all of that, I realize,

This story isn't finished. Not the writing. Not the living. There's a breath between today and tomorrow, a line left open, and somewhere beyond the horizon, in the quiet where love and faith hold hands, the next chapter is already waiting for me to write it. Still in love. Still here. Still unfinished. We are still. This is my story.

Acknowledgements

FROM CHARLES HAMILTON

There are stories we survive alone, and there are stories we survive because someone reached for our hand. My fight was never mine alone; it was ours. Ours to carry, ours to wrestle with, ours to overcome. My friends, my family, and my soulmate have been my anchor in the storm.

Although I know many have walked through similar fires, this is my story, personal, imperfect, and unrepeatable. I have learned that no one can pass through so many shadows and emerge unchanged. Some of us become quieter, some harder, some softer. I became all.

STILL, I AM HERE.

I want to thank a few people.

Grandma Erenstine, I had been gone for 15 years, and every day you cooked for me, and you prayed for me. At 98 years young, she loved me and welcomed me back into the family. I love you.

To **Brandon**, your note was not just a message, but a lifeline. You listened when I was silent, and you spoke when I could not. Your courage rewrote my ending and offered me a new beginning, which I never imagined.

To **Calvin** and his **wife**, thank you for seeing past my grief and gently nudging me toward life again. You reminded me that hope often arrives in the steady hands of friends.

To my **doctors and nurses**, thank you for treating me with dignity when I felt like a shadow of myself. For your hands, your patience, and the way you never flinched, I am forever grateful.

To my **co-workers**, thank you for stepping in when I was too sick to stand, for carrying my share when I could not.

To my **readers**, wherever you are, if you've loved and lost, felt yourself unravel, and somehow found the strength to rise again, this book was written for you. May you discover your own *still* in the quiet after the storm.

To my **mother and father**, I hope my work and my life honor your name. I miss you every day. In my sickness, I felt like a child calling for you, and though you were gone, you were here. My heart aches still.

And finally, to **God**, the Author of it all, who met me in the silence, in the pain, and the pause. Thank you for not letting the story end when I thought it should.

This was a difficult book to write, but even more challenging to live. Thank you for joining me along the way. I hope that somewhere within these words, you found a piece of yourself. At some point, we all will go on this journey.

Still

— Charles Hamilton

A Letter to My Younger Self

Dear Younger Self,

There will be moments when you feel alone, but remember, it's only a feeling. There will be moments when your voice grows louder than your imagination, but don't cling to them. Your voice is not for applause; it is meant to serve others. Be the voice for the voiceless. Question everything, even if it means sacrificing your comfort. The truth will always be the truth.

Be still. Listen more than you speak. Do not be afraid. You will lose people, but through loss, you will gain your voice. That voice, the one that spills between blank lines and empty spaces, will become your compass. Let God guide the pen.

It will be hard, but dream anyway. Dream the kind of dreams that scare you. Build from your imagination. Defy the very limits of reality. And love. Love the idea of love, because it will shape you. This gift of yours will take time to mature, but it will be lighter if you're not walking alone. Don't expect your partner to live inside your head; it's your sanctuary, not theirs. People will fear what they don't understand, and sometimes they will destroy what they fear.

Love will be your greatest investment, costlier than any home, more valuable than any treasure. It can make you believe you can change the world, and it can break you until you're certain you cannot go on. But fear not, God will send a voice to steady you in the dark. His name will be Genesis.

Remember, your mission is not to change people. It is to offer them another way of seeing. Know who you are.

Still
— *Charles Hamilton*

Epilogue – Still

The storms have passed, but I still feel the wind. It's softer now, a gentle breeze carrying voices of the past. Their moans, still unhealed, have anchored themselves in the shadows, hoping my "still" will dissolve into silence.

I am no longer the man I was when this journey began, but I am not yet the man I will become. That's the strange beauty of survival: it leaves you unfinished, suspended between the pain that shaped you and the peace that is shaping you still.

Some mornings, I wake without remembering the weight of my mortality. Other days, the echoes in my head return, sharp, clear, and intent on unlocking doors I sealed with heartbreak and tears. I no longer fear those echoes. They are proof that I lived through something worth remembering. My pain was not wasted.

I have learned that healing is not an ending, it is a beginning. The storms will come again; the winds will howl, and shadows will speak. But when they do, I will stand still.

You and I have walked this road together, you, dear reader, and I. And because of that, I want to give you the truth of what came next.

Rev. Franklin, my friend of over forty years, was there for me through so much. But our story ended in smoke. Age did not quiet his appetite for women, and after my separation from Karen, he began speaking to her behind my back, encouraging her in the story she told herself about leaving me. He forgot I was his friend, and I could not forget that betrayal.

Karen, in time, tried to return. She told me, "If two people love each other, there's nothing they couldn't resolve." I told her I hoped she found someone who loved her, but that someone could never be me.

Other loves remain in my life—Marie and my former wives—women who stood by me when life turned cold, as I did for them. Marie is still my counselor and my sparring partner; we disagree about nearly everything, but our friendship is unshakable.

And then there is Lucy, the one who walked back into the fire, not because she had to, but because love called her name. She is my echo, my silence, my shelter, my storm, and the unfinished sentence I have been writing all my life. I may never understand the grace that returned her to me, but I will spend my days trying to be worthy of it.

This book exists because I set aside another one, "Questions," waiting for its time. I believe that time is still coming. For now, this journey, our journey, is the one that needs to be told.

I hope that somewhere between these blank lines and empty spaces, you find your own "still." That you, too, can stand in the quiet after your storms and breathe without fear.

I am the ink. I am the pen. I am the words. I am you. And I live—still.

— *Charles Hamilton*

About the Author

Charles Hamilton writes from the fragile edge where survival meets grace. His words echo with lived experience: storms endured, silence carried, and the unbreakable thread of love that binds us back to life.

Born with a pen in his hand and questions in his heart, Hamilton has dedicated his life to seeking meaning in blank lines and empty spaces. His writing, deeply personal yet universally relatable, encourages readers to face pain, embrace resilience, and find the quiet strength that comes from stillness.

When not writing, he reflects on history, love, and the shared humanity that connects us all. It is still not just his story; it is an offering to anyone who has ever been broken and found a way to remain.